Women are repeatedly accused of taking things personally. I cannot see any other honest way of taking them.

—MARYA MANNES, b. 1904
American writer

a woman's notebook

Being a blank book
with quotes by women

I took a deep breath and listened to the old brag of my heart. I am, I am, I am.

—SYLVIA PLATH (1932–1963)
American poet

The moment of change is the only poem.

—ADRIENNE RICH, b. 1929
American poet

It's the frames which make some things important and some things forgotten. It's all only frames from which the content rises.

—EVE BABITZ, b. 1942
American writer

The universe is made of stories, not of atoms.

—MURIEL RUKEYSER (1913–1980)
American poet

Education is a private matter between the person and the world of knowledge and experience, and has little to do with school or college.

—**LILLIAN SMITH** (1897–1966)
American writer

As far as I'm concerned, being any gender is a drag.

—PATTI SMITH, b. 1943
American singer

The basic discovery about any people is the discovery of the relationship between its men and women.

—PEARL S. BUCK (1892–1973)
American writer

I thought that the chief thing to be done in order to equal boys was to be learned and courageous. So I decided to study Greek and learn to manage a horse.

—ELIZABETH CADY STANTON (1815–1902)
American suffragist

In my sex fantasy, nobody ever loves me for my mind.

—**NORA EPHRON**, b. 1941
American journalist

In passing, also, I would like to say that the first time Adam had a chance he laid the blame on woman.

—**NANCY ASTOR** (1879–1964)
British politician

Beauty is in the eye of the beholder.

—MARGARET WOLFE HUNGERFORD (1850–1897)
Irish novelist

Woman's virtue is man's greatest invention.

—CORNELIA OTIS SKINNER (1901–1979)
American writer

I only said, "I want to be let alone!"

—GRETA GARBO, b. 1905
Swedish actress

There are only two or three human stories, and they go on repeating themselves as fiercely as if they had never happened before.

—**WILLA CATHER** (1873–1947)
American writer

Nothing is more revealing than movement.

—MARTHA GRAHAM, b. 1894
American choreographer

My creed is low, be sincere and don't fuss.

—**JANE ADDAMS** (1860–1935)
American social worker

Courage is the price that Life exacts for granting peace.

—**AMELIA EARHART** (1898–1937)
American aviator

The world is born; wind, let it endure!

—**SIMONE WEIL** (1910–1943)
French writer

A scheme of which every part promises delight can never be successful; and general disappointment is only warded off by the defence of some little peculiar vexation.

—**JANE AUSTEN** (1775–1817)
English novelist

Noble deeds and hot baths are the best cures for depression.

—DODIE SMITH, b. 1896
English playwright

When choosing between two evils, I always like to try the one I've never tried before.

—**MAE WEST**, b. 1892
American actress

Here's a rule I recommend. Never practice two vices at once.
—**TALLULAH BANKHEAD** (1903–1968)
American actress

There is more difference within the sexes than between them.

—IVY COMPTON-BURNETT (1892–1969)
English satirist

There is only one sex.... A man and a woman are so entirely the same thing that one can scarcely understand the subtle reasons for sex distinction with which our minds are filled.

—GEORGE SAND (1804–1876)
French writer

The human Body is wondrously design'd,
But not as Habitation for
the human Mind!

—SAMANTHA FRANKLIN (1852–1879)
American pioneer

Whether women are better than men I cannot say—but I can say they are certainly no worse.

—**GOLDA MEIR** (1898–1978)
Israeli stateswoman

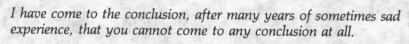

I have come to the conclusion, after many years of sometimes sad experience, that you cannot come to any conclusion at all.

—VITA SACKVILLE-WEST (1892–1962),
English writer

The human mind always makes progress, but it is a progress in spirals.

—MADAME DE STAEL (1766–1817)
French novelist

One learns in life to keep silent and draws one's own confusions.

—CORNELIA OTIS SKINNER (1901–1979)
American writer

Gentlemen always seem to remember blondes.

—ANITA LOOS, b. 1893
American writer

The way to a man's heart is through his stomach.

—**FANNY FERN** (1811–1872)
American writer

Progress in civilization has been accompanied by progress in cookery.

—FANNIE FARMER (1857–1915)
American cooking teacher

Eternity is not something that begins after you are dead. It is going on all the time. We are in it now.

—CHARLOTTE PERKINS GILMAN (1860–1935)
American writer

"But it's always interesting when one doesn't see," she added. "If you don't see what a thing means, you must be looking at it wrong way round."

—**AGATHA CHRISTIE** (1891–1978)
English mystery writer

The wave of the future is coming and there is no stopping it.

—ANNE MORROW LINDBERGH, b. 1906
American writer

The only thing that makes life possible is permanent, intolerable uncertainty: not knowing what comes next.

—URSULA K. LE GUIN, b. 1929
American writer

On this narrow planet, we have only the choice between two unknown worlds.

—**COLETTE** (1873–1954)
French writer

Thus strangely are our souls constructed, and by such slight ligaments are we bound to prosperity or ruin.

—**MARY SHELLEY** (1797–1851)
English writer

I am always running into peoples' unconscious.

—MARILYN MONROE (1926–1962)
American actress

I hate
this wretched willow soul of mine,
patiently enduring, plaited or twisted
by other hands.

—KARIN BOYE (1900–1941)
Swedish poet

Energy is the power that drives every human being. It is not lost by exertion but maintained by it.

—GERMAINE GREER, b. 1939
Australian writer

I have willed to go forward and have not
advanced beyond
the borders of my grave.

—SANIYA SALIH, b. 1939
Syrian poet

It is not true that life is one damn thing after another—it's one damn thing over and over.

—EDNA ST. VINCENT MILLAY (1892–1952)
American poet

It is always one's virtues and not one's vices that precipitate one into disaster.

—REBECCA WEST, b. 1892
British writer

It was so cold I almost got married.

—SHELLEY WINTERS, b. 1922
American actress

One never notices what has been done; one can only see what remains to be done.

—MARIE CURIE (1867–1934)
French scientist

Character builds slowly, but it can be torn down with incredible swiftness.

—**FAITH BALDWIN** (1893–1978)
American writer

I began to have an idea of my life, not as the slow shaping of achievement to fit my preconceived purposes, but as the gradual discovery and growth of a purpose which I did not know.

—JOANNA FIELD, b. 1900
English psychologist

Marriage removes the illusion, deeply imbedded previously, that somewhere there is a soul-mate.

—PAULA MODERSOHN-BECKER (1876–1907)
German painter

And when her biographer says of an Italian woman poet, "during some years her Muse was intermitted," we do not wonder at the fact when he casually mentions her ten children.

—**ANNA GARLIN SPENCER** (1851–1931)
American social reformer

She might struggle like a fly in a web. He wrapped her around and around with beautiful sentences.

—MARY CATHERWOOD (1847–1901)
American writer

Nobody can make you feel
inferior without your consent.

—ELEANOR ROOSEVELT (1884–1962)
American stateswoman

Elegance has a bad effect on my constitution.
—LOUISA MAY ALCOTT (1832–1888)
American writer

I was a fantastic student until ten, and then my mind began to wander.

—GRACE PALEY, b. 1922
American writer

Some set more by such things as come from a distance, but I rec'lect mother always used to maintain that folks was meant to be doctored with the stuff that grew right about 'em.

—SARAH ORNE JEWETT (1849–1909)
American writer

Look not earnestly at any other that is eating.
When moderately satisfied leave the table.
Sing not, hum not, wriggle not.

—ALICE MORSE EARL (1853–1911)
American writer

Science may carry us to Mars, but it will leave the earth peopled as ever by the inept.

—**AGNES REPPLIER** (1858–1950)
American writer

A difference of taste in jokes is a great strain on the affections.

—GEORGE ELIOT (1819–1880)
English writer

Some minds remain open long enough for the truth not only to enter but to pass on through by way of a ready exit without pausing anywhere along the route.

—ELIZABETH KENNY (1886–1952)
Australian nurse

Be fond of the man who jests at his scars, if you like; but never believe he is being on the level with you.

—**PAMELA HANSFORD JOHNSON**, b. 1912
English writer

When people envy me, I think, oh, God, don't envy me. I have my own pains.

—BARBRA STREISAND, b. 1942
American entertainer

Do we really know anybody? Who does not wear one face to hide another?

—**FRANCES MARION** (1886–1973)
American journalist

Memory in America suffers amnesia.

—MERIDEL LE SUEUR, b. 1900
American historian

A broken heart is what makes life so wonderful five years later, when you see the guy in an elevator and he is fat and smoking a cigar and saying long-time-no-see. If he hadn't broken your heart, you couldn't have that glorious feeling of relief!

—PHYLLIS BATTELLE, b. 1922
American journalist

General notions are generally wrong.
—LADY MARY WORTLEY MONTAGU (1689–1762)
English writer

The perfect hostess will see to it that the works of male and female authors be properly separated on her bookshelves. Their proximity, unless the authors happen to be married, should not be tolerated.

—LADY COUGH'S ETIQUETTE (1863)

She did observe, with some dismay, that, far from conquering all,
love lazily sidestepped practical problems.

—JEAN STAFFORD (1915–1979)
American writer

No man can be held throughout the day by what happens throughout the night.

—SALLY STANFORD, b. 1904
American madam

How idiotic civilization is! Why be given a body if you have to keep it shut up in a case like a rare, rare fiddle?

—KATHERINE MANSFIELD (1888–1923)
English writer

No matter what your fight, don't be ladylike! God Almighty made
women and the Rockefeller gang of thieves made the ladies.

—"MOTHER" MARY JONES (1830–1930)
American labor organizer

"Will you walk into my parlour?" said a spider to a fly.

—MARY HOWITT (1799–1888)
British writer

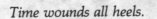

Time wounds all heels.

—**JANE ACE** (1905–1974)
American radio personality

I have often wished I had time to cultivate modesty.... But I am too busy thinking about myself.

—EDITH SITWELL (1887–1964)
English poet

I never hated a man enough to give him diamonds back.

—ZSA ZSA GABOR, b. 1923
Hungarian actress

The idea of perfection always gives one a chance to talk without knowing the facts.

—AGNES SLIGH TURNBULL, b. 1888
American writer

In real love you want the other person's good. In romantic love you want the other person.

—MARGARET ANDERSON (1893–1973)
American publisher

Flawless mental sight! That is genius.

— MAUDE ADAMS (1872–1953)
American actress

The best impromptu speeches are the ones written well in advance.

—RUTH GORDON, b. 1896
American actress

It doesn't matter what you do in the bedroom as long as you don't do it in the street and frighten the horses.

—MRS. PATRICK CAMPBELL (1865–1940)
English actress

The great power and privilege I had foregone of earning money by my own labor occurred to me.

—FRANCES ANNE KEMBLE (1809–1893)
English writer

A caress is better than a career.
—ELISABETH MARBURY (1856–1933)
American theatrical agent

To have one's individuality completely ignored is like being pushed quite out of life. Like being blown out as one blows out a light.

—EVELYN SCOTT (1893–1963)
American writer

Her family, she thought, was like this room: too comfortable, too hot, and far too crowded.

—PENELOPE MORTIMER, b. 1918
English writer

Family jokes, though rightly cursed by strangers, are the bond that keeps most families alive.

—STELLA BENSON (1892–1933)
English writer

The soufflé is the misunderstood woman of the culinary world.

—IRMA S. ROMBAUER (1877–1962)
American cook

Constant togetherness is fine—but only for Siamese twins.

—VICTORIA BILLINGS, b. 1945
American journalist

Ah! Those strange people who have the courage to be unhappy!
Are they unhappy, by-the-way?

—ALICE JAMES (1848–1892)
American diarist

No mockery in the world ever sounds to me as hollow as that of being told to cultivate happiness....Happiness is not a potato, to be planted in mould, and tilled with manure.

—CHARLOTTE BRONTE (1816–1855)
English writer

Fiction reveals truths that reality obscures.

—JESSAMYN WEST, b. 1907
American writer

Why does a slight tax increase cost you two hundred dollars and a substantial tax cut save you thirty cents?

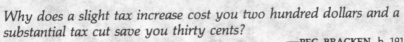

—PEG BRACKEN, b. 1918
American humorist

I like a view but I like to sit with my back turned to it.

—GERTRUDE STEIN (1874–1946)
American writer

Women have served all these centuries as looking-glasses possessing the magic and delicious power of reflecting the figure of man at twice its natural size.

—VIRGINIA WOOLF (1882–1941)
English writer

The trouble with being in the rat race is that even if you win, you're still a rat.

—LILY TOMLIN, b. 1939
American actress